The First Book of Broadway Solos

Part II

Compiled by Joan Frey Boytim

ISBN-13: 978-1-4234-2711-7
ISBN-10: 1-4234-2711-4

HAL•LEONARD®
CORPORATION

7777 W. BLUEMOUND RD. P.O. BOX 13819 MILWAUKEE, WI 53213

Visit Hal Leonard Online at
www.halleonard.com

Preface

Many voice teachers who have enjoyed using *The First Book of Broadway Solos* with students have asked me to compile more theatre music collections along the same lines. I am pleased to respond to this request with *The First Book of Broadway Solos–Part II*. I have purposely kept the choice of songs comparable to the ideas set forth in the original books. The collections address a traditional, classical voice teacher's sensibilities and needs in teaching basic techniques of lyric singing while using the music of Broadway.

The level is exactly the same for *The First Book of Broadway Solos* and *The First Book of Broadway Solos–Part II*. A student could begin in either book.

I feel it is important to repeat some of the ideas from the original Preface.

The songs in these collections were chosen for beginning voice students to assist in developing a solid technique during the first months or years of lessons. In most cases, the original voice category is preserved, although at times I chose, for musical and vocal reasons, to use a song originally sung by a baritone or tenor, for instance, in the mezzo-soprano collection. For those persons coming from a theatre point of view, it should be noted that these books are not designed for the belting style of singing. That is not to say that a more theatrical style of singing is not important in other contexts. But for the purposes of traditional vocal instruction, classically based, lyric singing is the aim of this series.

The songs are moderate in length and most of the accompaniments are more straight-forward and less elaborate than in the original show versions (in the complete vocal score of a show, or in *The Singer's Musical Theatre Anthology*). Many of the keys have been adjusted to a comfortable, modest range for each voice type.

Great thought went into choosing a companion body of songs that were suitable for teenage voices or beginning adults. There are plenty of familiar selections and some "showstoppers" that teens always want to sing, even if the songs are more adult in nature. Many interesting pieces from lesser known musicals are included for those who enjoy trying something different from the most popular songs.

These new volumes will provide some new study and performance choices for those who wish to include in their repertory the unique art form of musical theatre.

Joan Frey Boytim

The First Book of Broadway Solos
Part II

Pianist on the CD: Laura Ward

* London

In the accompaniment recordings of some songs, repeats are omitted.

BILL
from SHOW BOAT

Music by JEROME KERN
Words by P.G. WODEHOUSE and OSCAR HAMMERSTEIN II

BEAUTY AND THE BEAST

from Walt Disney's BEAUTY AND THE BEAST: THE BROADWAY MUSICAL

Lyrics by HOWARD ASHMAN
Music by ALAN MENKEN

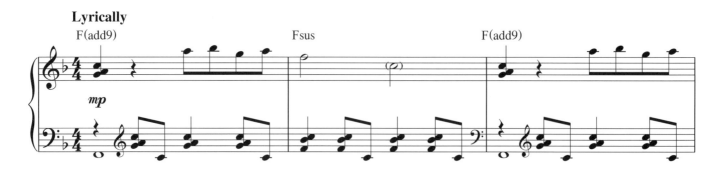

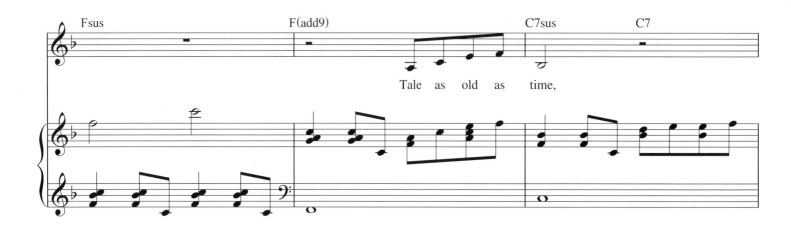

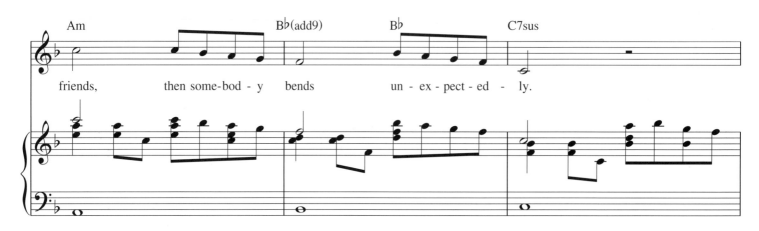

CASTLE ON A CLOUD
from LES MISÉRABLES

Music by CLAUDE-MICHEL SCHÖNBERG
Lyrics by ALAIN BOUBLIL, JEAN MARC NATEL
and HERBERT KRETZMER

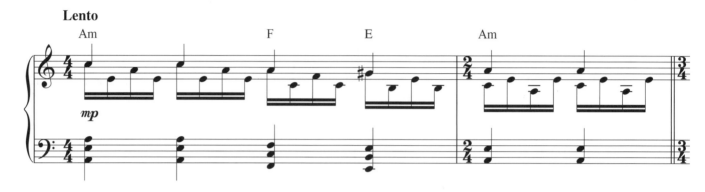

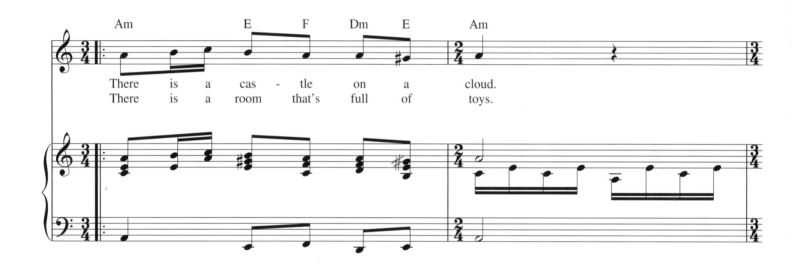

There is a cas - tle on a cloud.
There is a room that's full of toys.

I like to go there in my sleep.
There are a hun - dred boys and girls.

FEED THE BIRDS

from Walt Disney's MARY POPPINS

Words and Music by RICHARD M. SHERMAN
and ROBERT B. SHERMAN

Tempo I

HOW ARE THINGS IN GLOCCA MORRA

from FINIAN'S RAINBOW

Words by E.Y. "YIP" HARBURG
Music by BURTON LANE

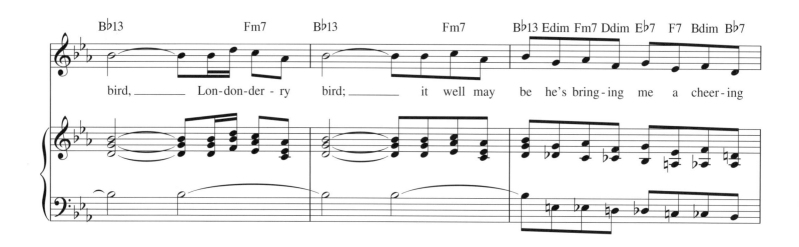

I CAIN'T SAY NO
from OKLAHOMA!

Lyrics by OSCAR HAMMERSTEIN II
Music by RICHARD RODGERS

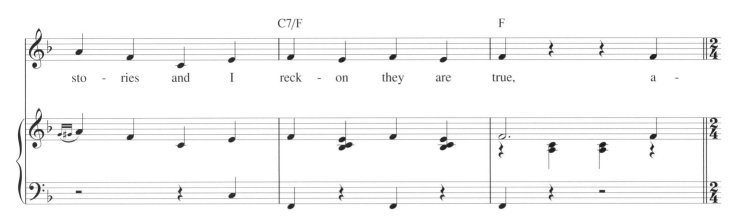

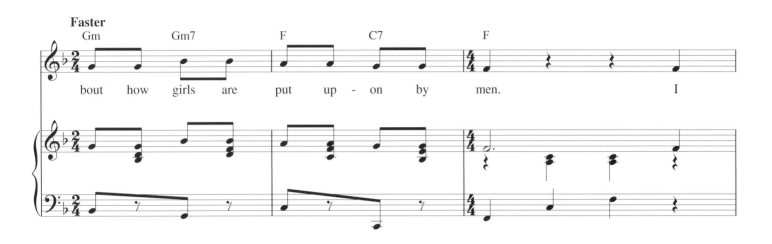

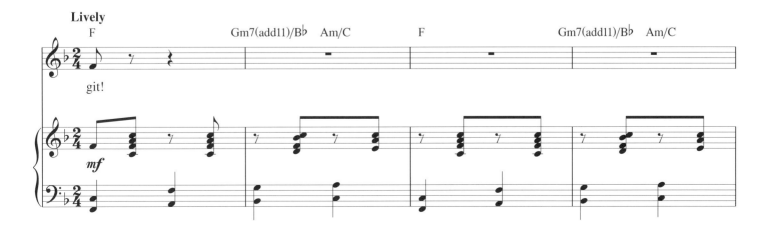

Refrain

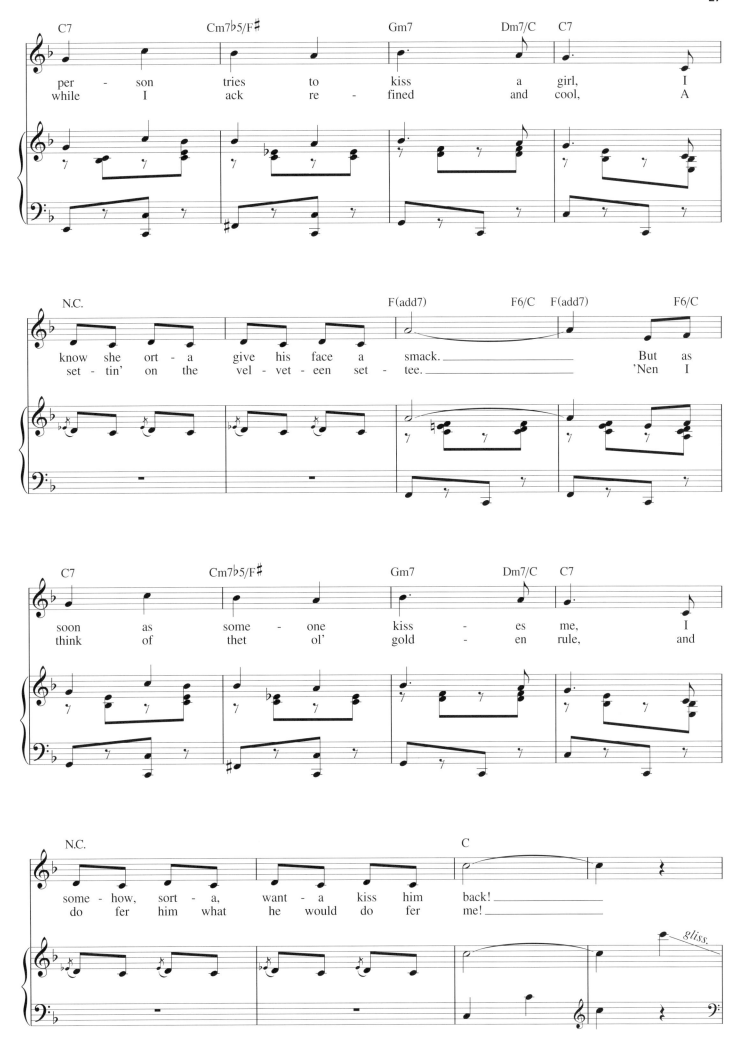

I NEVER KNEW HIS NAME

from THE CIVIL WAR: AN AMERICAN MUSICAL

Words by JACK MURPHY
Music by FRANK WILDHORN

I GOT THE SUN IN THE MORNING

from the Stage Production ANNIE GET YOUR GUN

Words and Music by
IRVING BERLIN

Allegro moderato

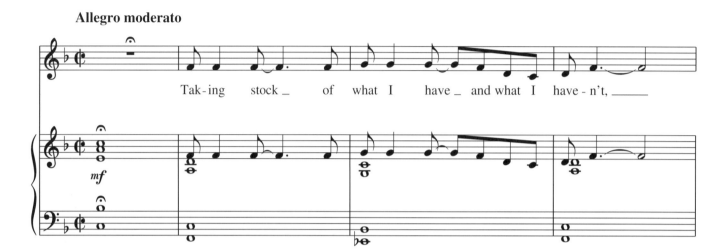

Tak-ing stock _ of what I have _ and what I have-n't, _____

What do I find? _ The things I have will keep me sat-is-fied. _____

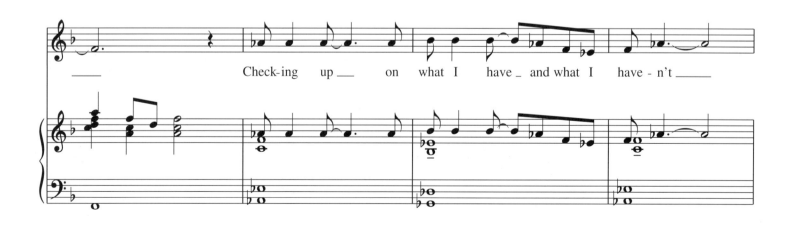

_____ Check-ing up _ on what I have _ and what I have-n't _____

Got no check-books, got no banks, _ Still I'd like _ to ex-
Got no heir-looms, for my kin, ____ Made no will _ but when

press my thanks, _ I got the } sun in the morn-ing and the moon at night. _____
I cash in ____ I'll leave the } sun in the morn-ing and the moon at night. _____

And with the sun in the morn-ing and the

moon in the eve-ning I'm ____ all right. right.

I'VE NEVER BEEN IN LOVE BEFORE

from GUYS AND DOLLS

By FRANK LOESSER

I LOVED YOU ONCE IN SILENCE

from CAMELOT

Words by ALAN JAY LERNER
Music by FREDERICK LOEWE

44

IN THE STILL OF THE NIGHT

from ROSALIE

Words and Music by
COLE PORTER

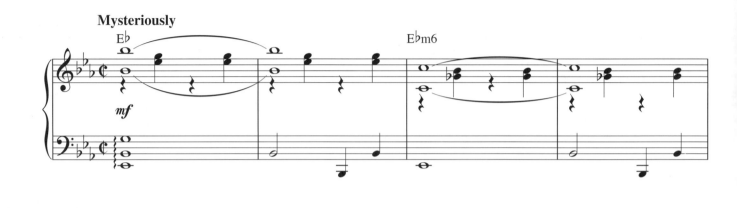

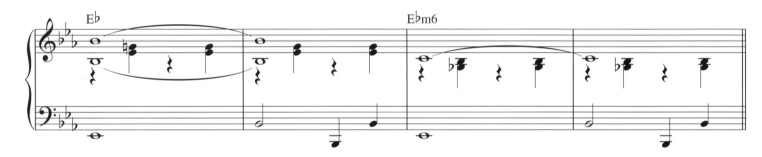

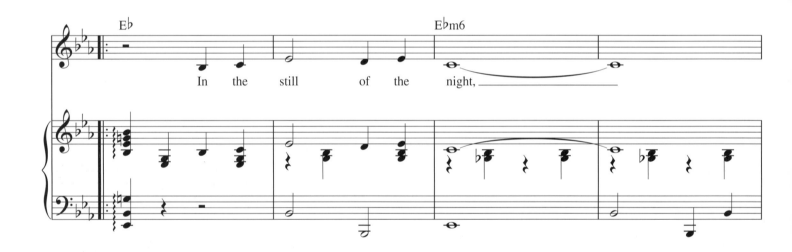

In the still of the night, _____

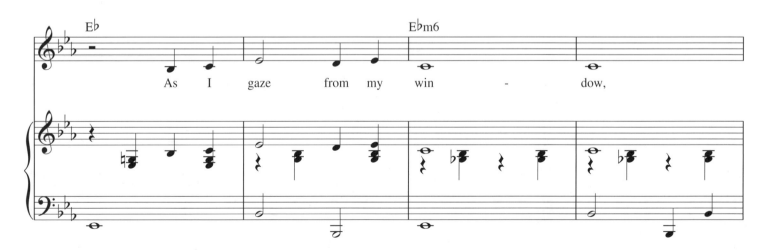

As I gaze from my win - dow,

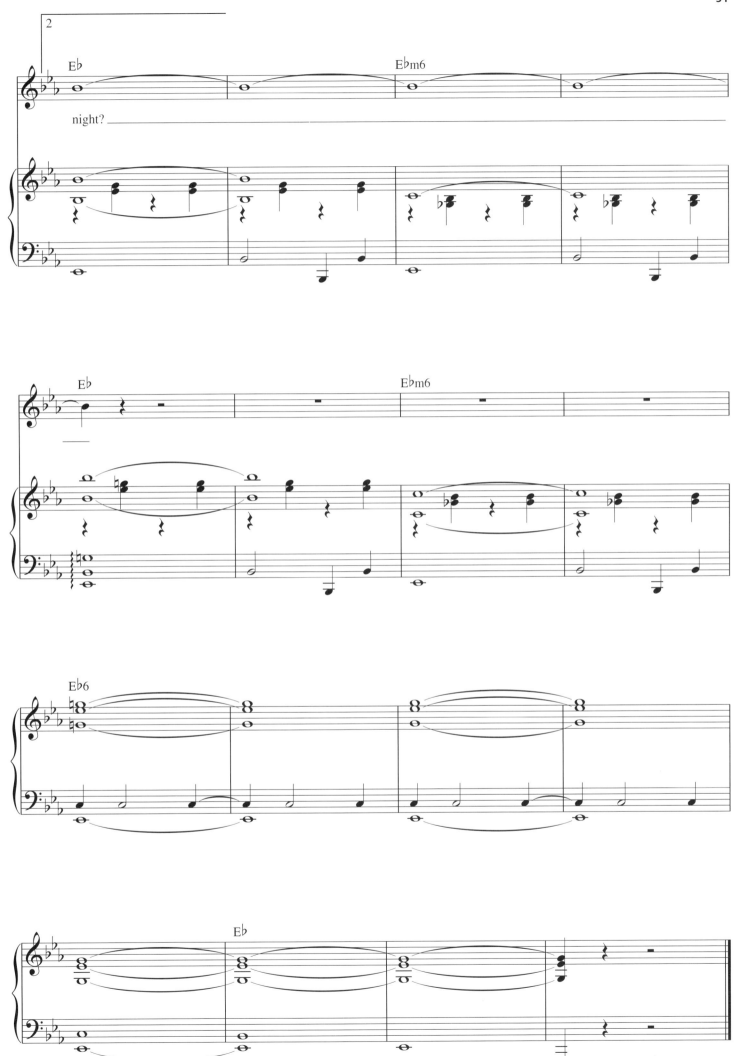

IS IT REALLY ME?

from 110 IN THE SHADE

Words by TOM JONES
Music by HARVEY SCHMIDT

LAZY AFTERNOON

from THE GOLDEN APPLE

Words and Music by JOHN LATOUCHE
and JEROME MOROSS

LOVE, DON'T TURN AWAY

from 110 IN THE SHADE

Words by TOM JONES
Music by HARVEY SCHMIDT

Vigorously

Refrain *(not too fast)*

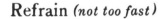

I have so man-y things I want to do for you.___ I have so man-y things saved up to say.___ I have

MATCHMAKER

from the Musical FIDDLER ON THE ROOF

Words by SHELDON HARNICK
Music by JERRY BOCK

MEMORY
from CATS

Music by ANDREW LLOYD WEBBER
Text by TREVOR NUNN after T.S. ELLIOT

Burnt out ends of smo - ky days, _____ the stale cold smell _____ of mor - ning. _____ The street lamp dies, an - o - ther night is ov - er, _____ an - o - ther day is dawn - ing.

poco rit.

poco rit.

Touch me._____ It's so ea - sy to leave me _____ All a - lone with the me - mory _____ Of my days in the sun. _____ If you touch me you'll un-der-stand what hap - pi-ness is. Look a new day has be - gun.

ONCE UPON A DREAM

from JEKYLL & HYDE

Words by STEVE CUDEN AND LESLIE BRICUSSE
Music by FRANK WILDHORN

SHALL WE DANCE?

from THE KING AND I

Lyrics by OSCAR HAMMERSTEIN II
Music by RICHARD RODGERS

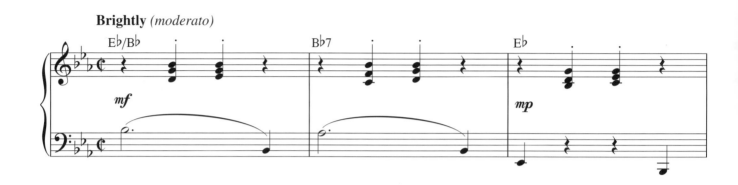

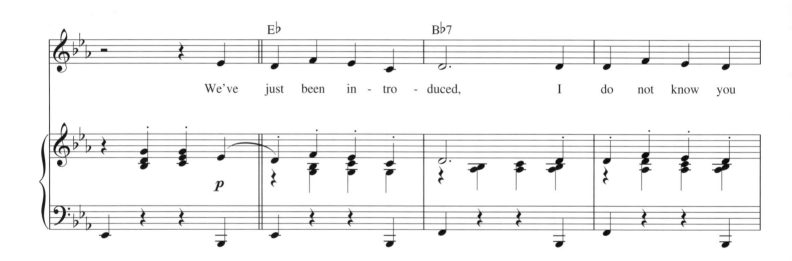

We've just been in-tro-duced, I do not know you well. But when the mu-sic start-ed, some-thing drew me to your side. So

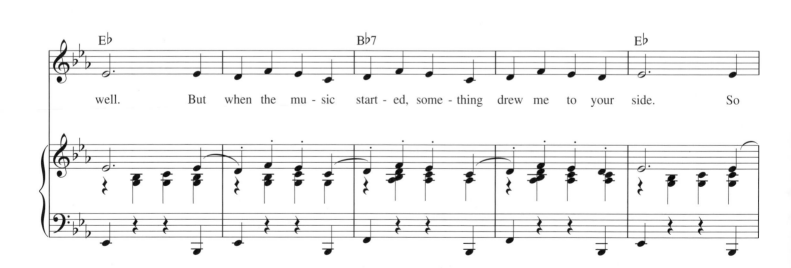

Shall we then say "good-night" and mean "good-bye?" Or, per - chance _____ when the last lit - tle star has left the sky. Shall we still be to - geth - er with our arms a - round each

STEPSISTERS'S LAMENT
from CINDERELLA

Lyrics by OSCAR HAMMERSTEIN II
Music by RICHARD RODGERS

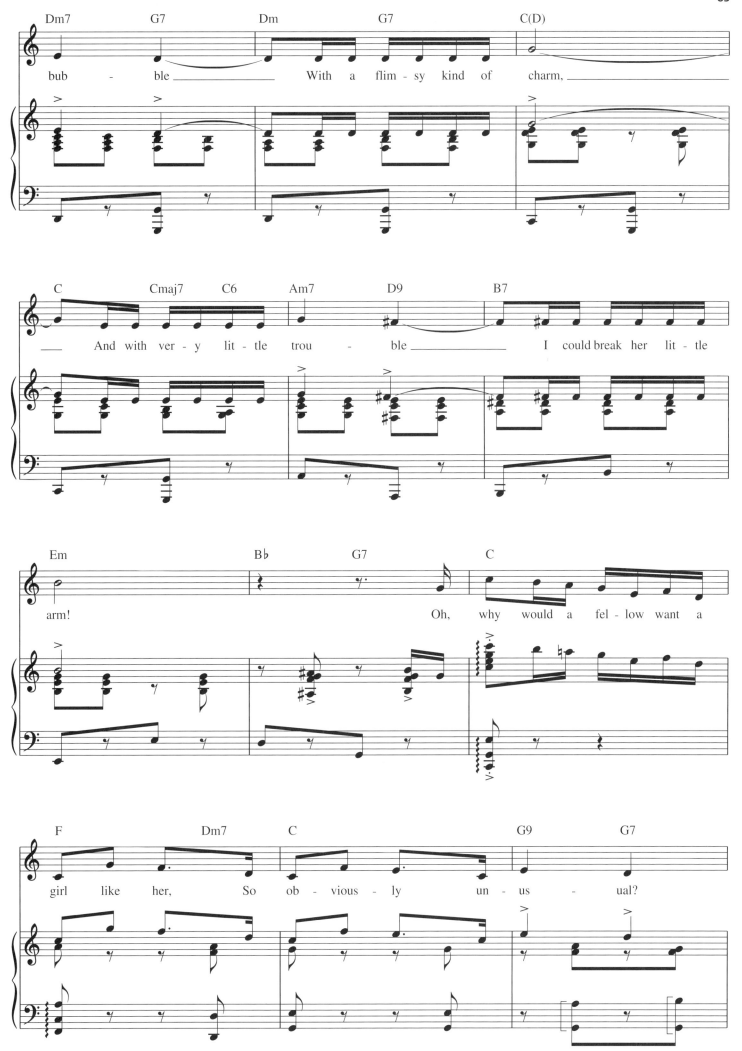

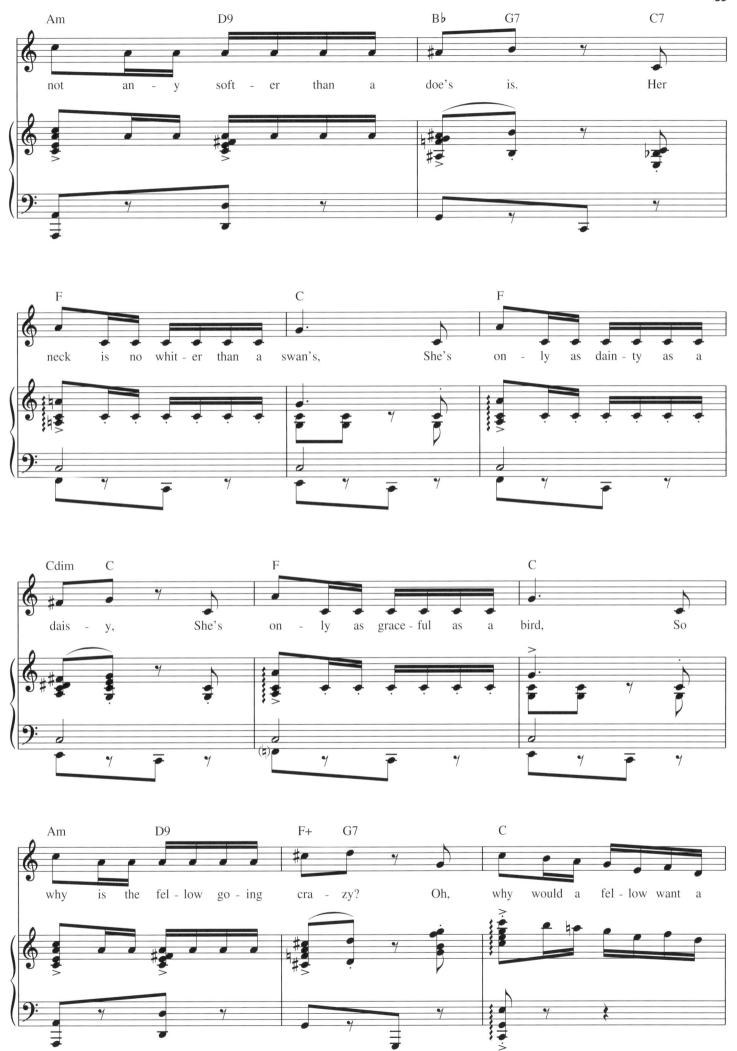

SYMPATHY, TENDERNESS

from JEKYLL & HYDE

Words by LESLIE BRICUSSE
Music by FRANK WILDHORN

THEY SAY IT'S WONDERFUL

from the Stage Production ANNIE GET YOUR GUN

Words and Music by
IRVING BERLIN

won - der - ful _____ so they tell me. _____ I

can't re - call who said it, I know I nev - er read it, I

on - ly know they tell me that love is grand, and,

the thing that's known as ro - mance is won - der - ful, won - der - ful,

in ev - 'ry way ___ So they say. ___ You leave your house some

morn - ing and with - out an - y warn - ing, you're stop - ping peo - ple shout - ing that love is

grand, and to hold a man in your arms is won - der - ful,

won - der - ful in ev - 'ry way, ___ so they say. ___

rit.

8vb

WHAT I DID FOR LOVE

from A CHORUS LINE

Music by MARVIN HAMLISCH
Lyric by EDWARD KLEBAN

WHISTLE DOWN THE WIND

from WHISTLE DOWN THE WIND

Music by ANDREW LLOYD WEBBER
Lyrics by JIM STEINMAN

Moderato con moto

Whis-tle down the wind, _____ let your voic-es car-ry _____ drown out all the rain, light a patch of dark-ness, treach-er-ous and scar-y. _____ Howl at the stars, _____

VIOLETS AND SILVERBELLS

Reprise
from SHENANDOAH

Lyric by PETER UDELL
Music by GARY GELD

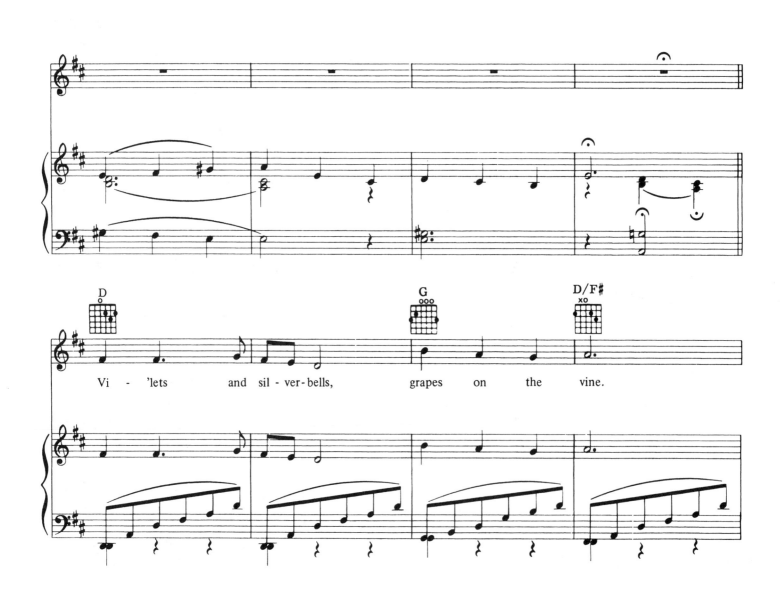